ENCOMP

David Adam

To Denise, whose love and sharing
makes my writing possible

First published in Great Britain in 2014

Society for Promoting Christian Knowledge
36 Causton Street
London SW1P 4ST
www.spckpublishing.co.uk

Unless otherwise noted, Scripture quotations are taken from the New Revised Standard
Version of the Bible, Anglicized Edition, copyright © 1989, 1995 by the Division of
Christian Education of the National Council of the Churches of Christ in
the USA. Used by permission. All rights reserved.
The extract marked KJV is taken from the Authorized Version of the Bible (The King
James Bible), the rights in which are vested in the Crown, and is reproduced
by permission of the Crown's Patentee, Cambridge University Press.

The publisher and author acknowledge with thanks permission to reproduce
extracts from the following:
Common Worship: Daily Prayer is copyright © The Archbishops' Council, 2005,
and extracts are reproduced by permission. <copyright@c-of-e.org.uk>
'Circle me, O God' and 'You are the caller', from David Adam, *The Edge of Glory*
(SPCK/Triangle, 1985), are copyright © SPCK and are reproduced by permission.
Every effort has been made to acknowledge fully the sources of material reproduced in
this book. The publisher apologizes for any omissions that may remain and, if notified,
will ensure that full acknowledgements are made in a subsequent edition.

British Library Cataloguing-in-Publication Data
A catalogue record for this book is available from the British Library

ISBN 978–0–281–07058–9
eBook ISBN 978–0–281–07059–6

Typeset by Graphicraft Limited, Hong Kong
Manufacture managed by Jellyfish
Printed in Great Britain by CPI
Subsequently digitally printed in Great Britain

eBook by Graphicraft Limited, Hong Kong

Produced on paper from sustainable forests

Contents

———•◆•———

You encompass me behind and before
and lay your hand upon me.
Such knowledge is too wonderful for me,
so high that I cannot attain it.

(Psalm 139.4–5,
Common Worship: Daily Prayer)

Acknowledgements

I would like to thank SPCK for its continued support, and for allowing me to use prayers from my first book, *The Edge of Glory*. Among the staff of SPCK, I am especially grateful to Alison Barr for her continued friendship and guidance, and to Monica Capoferri and (former staff member) Nikki Bovis-Coulter, whose illustrations add an extra dimension to what I have written. I am indebted to the many groups that have shared in my experimenting with prayers, in particular to the churches of Castleton and Danby in North Yorkshire, where my writing of prayers really began. Finally, none of this would be possible without the love, support and encouragement of my wife Denise.

Introduction

———•◦•———

Encompassing God is not about what we do but about what God is doing all the time. God holds us and all creation in his loving embrace: there is not anywhere or anything without God. This book aims to encourage people to give their attention to this reality, to become aware of it, to affirm it, and to rejoice in the presence of God. We need to discover the joy that 'we abide in him and he in us' (1 John 4.13).

God encompasses us whether we notice this or choose to ignore it. Just as the air is about us and within us, God's presence surrounds and fills us. We are all immersed in him: those who are baptized and those who are not; Christians, Jews, Muslims, people of other faiths and people of none. But though God is in us, he is not ours to possess. The Church does not have a monopoly on God and cannot cage him in its buildings or its dogma, though it has often tried to.

We cannot bring God to another person, because he is already within every one of us – as much with the criminal as he is with the bishop, though each can fail to notice him. We can, however, help each other discover God's presence. And sometimes we find that God's presence is revealed to us by someone else. I can remember once many years ago thinking that I would take God to a parishioner who was ill. Well, I found that God was there long before I arrived! He had been with this elderly, frail lady for such a length of time that they were friends and she was more relaxed in his presence than I was. She could say 'The Lord is here' with a joyful affirmation in all her troubles.

As God is with us and within us, there is no need to search for him, though we do need to learn how to attune ourselves to his presence. In our modern world, sound waves and television images are always around but we need to tune in our digital TV to hear and see them. In a similar way, we need to learn how to turn our attention to God and to rejoice in his presence, as we take the great journey of discovery to know that 'In him we live and move and have our being' (Acts 17.28).

The writing of this book was born to some degree out of frustration. I will be mentioning some of the issues that have bothered me regarding our modes of worship and how we express God's presence. I would then like to offer you a way of praying that I believe will help you personally to consider the pace you live at and to explore how you may deepen your worship. We will also look at outreach to others and the part we can play in helping those who sit in darkness and the shadow of death to become aware that God *is* actually with them and loves them.

All through my ministry, I've been fortunate to be involved with groups of teenagers and young adults who want to grow in the faith. Often, when I was curate in West Auckland and Hartlepool, I would be told that the services were difficult, if not plain dull. Yet all concerned were sure that God is not dull – the vicar and the curate could be, but God never! These young folk were looking for ways of exploring the wonder of the presence of God and the reality of his love. I am passionate about the services of Matins, Holy Communion and Evensong, and I find great depths in the Psalms. But to present these to new Christians as the way to God is like taking them into a gallery of Old Masters and expecting them to enjoy the riches of art immediately. No age can simply live off past glories; it also needs to communicate in a way that is meaningful for its own time. I knew I had to experiment with worship and find new expressions of the liturgy.

At various stages of our lives, we will find that different forms of worship help keep us aware that we are in God's presence and grace. We should not feel too tightly tied to the words in a book, but rather allow ourselves to be touched by the power of God they reveal. Sometimes, in awe, my young folk and I would move into deep silence where we would remain receptive and open to the reality that we are one in him. At other times we would be led into joyful singing of God's praise.

I believe there is a great need to restore in our services the balance between speech and silence, action and stillness, so that we allow time for God to communicate with us. So many of our services run to a fixed agenda and are crammed with activity. God scarcely gets a look-in! We offer people words, when what they want is the Word made flesh. We use formulas without ever helping people to rejoice in what we convey. For example, services often start with 'In the name of the Father, and of the Son, and of the Holy Spirit', followed by 'The Lord be with you: and also with you', or something similar. In about 20 seconds we have uttered great wonders without pause for breath or thought. I have more than once suggested we need no more words than these, for if we recognize their true meaning, we'll go home rejoicing, with the depth of what has been said vibrating in our lives. Such words should be able to open the eyes of the blind, and make people aware that they are in God's presence. Such words should remind people of their baptism and that they are immersed in the very being of God: we dwell in him. When we use these opening words, have we rested in the presence, in the peace, in the power of God? Have we spent time joyously abiding in the light, in the love, in the leading of God? Were those fleeting seconds communicating that we are truly in the goodness, the grace and the guiding of God: that we are in the strength, in the salvation, in the seeking of God? Did we rejoice in the reality that the Lord *is* here? Was our God allowed to get a word in before the notices or a hymn? Enough questions! Take your time to abide in him now. Stop and rejoice 'In the name of the Father and of the Son and of the Holy Spirit', in the very presence and power of your God, who is with you, about you and within you.

In prayer, what is more important than what we are doing is what God is doing to us, with us and through us. I saw a sticker on a car windscreen once that said, 'Prayer makes God jump'. I noticed there was an L-plate just below the sticker and hoped the driver would learn more about who is at work in our prayers. Prayer is not about making God do, for that would be magic, but about opening our lives to the ever-present God so that he can work in us and through us. Intercession begins by perceiving that we are created by God and encompassed by him. All true intercession is dependent on this recognition and indwelling.

Prayer is as much about the space between the words as the words themselves: it is about being aware of the Holy One in our midst. We shape who we are by the attitudes we have, by the patterns we create for ourselves. Not only prayer, but life and work too are less irksome if we discover we are working with the Holy One who dwells with us as we dwell in him. In prayer, do we make room for each word to resonate or do we speed onto the next one? The faster we go, the less we truly see what is and who is about us. Give each word, each space, each comma, each full stop the attention it is due and allow yourself to be tuned to God's presence. God is not absent from us but we are absent from him when we stand in his presence and ignore him. We are caught talking about and talking to God but failing to listen to or be fully aware of him. Worship

4

is not of the mind alone; it is an act of devotion. Prayer is about heart-to-heart speaking and listening, which allows space for the other to speak too. We need to leave room in our worship for reverence, receptivity and the reception of our God: this can lead to the revelation that 'Surely the LORD is in this place – and I did not know it!' (Genesis 28.16). Eternity is not beyond us, nor is it only available after death. It is here and now in the presence of God, and he awaits our awareness and our rejoicing in him. God is not the object of our prayers but the subject, and prayer begins with the removal of all obstacles that prevent him communicating with us. We don't want an obsession with formulas, ideas or techniques to make us lose sight of the reality that prayer is about God at work in our lives and in the world. Stillness and space give us the opportunity to become more open to him, and focusing our attention fully on God is nothing less than life-transfiguring.

Having said this, I believe that there is great value to be found in recitation and repetition, for these help us enter into the essence of what is being said. Recitation allows words to vibrate on our lips and ears, while in repetition we seek to let them vibrate in our lives: we hold them in our hearts; we ponder them in our inner being. As words gain a new depth, a single term or phrase can bring us to a profound awareness of the riches it points to. Words are not relics of the past: they may have a great history but they can be new and fresh and meaningful for us and help us grow. In worship we should be ready to be changed, to be transfigured, and to be thrilled by the sacredness of all life and the holiness of every place, for the Lord is here and his Spirit is with us.

To help deepen people's awareness of God, I've often used the first 11 verses of Psalm 139, which is a prayer that looks at God in six different directions. Read the Psalm slowly and see if you discover them.

O Lord, you have searched me out and known me;
you know my sitting down and my rising up;
you discern my thoughts from afar.
You mark out my journeys and my resting place
and are acquainted with all my ways.
For there is not a word on my tongue,
but you, O Lord, know it altogether.
You encompass me behind and before
and lay your hand upon me.
Such knowledge is too wonderful for me,
so high that I cannot attain it.
Where can I go then from your spirit?
Or where can I flee from your presence?
If I climb up to heaven, you are there;
if I make the grave my bed, you are there also.
If I take the wings of the morning
and dwell in the uttermost parts of the sea,
Even there your hand shall lead me,
your right hand hold me fast.
If I say, 'Surely the darkness will cover me
and the light around me turn to night,'
Even the darkness is no darkness with you;
the night is as clear as the day;
darkness and light are to you both alike.

> (*Common Worship Daily Prayer*,
> Church House Publishing, 2005)

Did you find each of the directions? If not, go over the psalm
again. Now notice that the psalmist begins by addressing God
and assuming his presence. This same God is present with you
and you could apply the 'facts' of this psalm (below) to yourself.
Read through each verse of the psalm with God, not just in
word but by resting in his presence. Then look at the list of

facts. Say 'God', leave a short pause, then contemplate one line and pause for a minute or so. Now say out loud the verse the fact relates to (given at the end of each line) and the fact itself. This act of affirmation should take 20 minutes at least. It is a good way of tuning into how God encompasses you, and is with you wherever you are.

THE FACTS

God, you know me and my thoughts. 139.1
God, you know where I am. 139.2–3
God, you know all I say. 139.4
God, you encompass me. 139.5
God, you are before me. 139.4–5
God, you are behind me 139.4–5
God, you are beyond my understanding. 139.5
God, there is nowhere without you. 139.6
God, you are above me. 139.7
God, you are beneath me. 139.7
God, you are on my right. 139.8–9
God, you are on my left. 139.8–9
God, you are with me even in my darkness. 139.10–11

This meditation on the wonder of being in the presence of the Almighty expresses the relationship between God and us. We are the 'object' of God's action. It is primarily God who is at work and we rejoice in, and affirm, his activity in our lives. In line after line, God and self are woven together, emphasizing that we don't just know about God but know him, as he knows us. God is always there, not in a threatening way like a police-man watching in judgement, but as a lover who is a ready help, a strength and support.

God's knowledge of you is comprehensive. He knows your sitting down and your rising up, your thoughts, your journeys, your places of rest, and all that you say. 'You have searched me out' means 'you have dug deep into the depths of me and know me fully'. This is not a surface looking at but the deep familiarity of a relationship. It is intimate knowledge: God looks at you with the eyes of love: he knows the real you, and though he knows you fully, he still lays his hand upon you in blessing (139.1–4).

The knowledge of such a presence and love should fill you with wonder and awe. It is actually more than you can take in or put into words, but you can experience it in your life nevertheless (139.5).

God is present wherever you are, whatever your situation. If you find yourself rising up in joy, if all is going well with you, if you feel you are in heaven, God is there. If you descend to the depths, if life seems like the pits, like hell or you feel as good as dead, God is still with you. He never leaves you (Psalm 139.6–7).

Go as far as you can go to the east: God is still there at the beginning of each morning, there at its dawning, even if it is dull and stormy. You can communicate with God at the start of each day. Or go as far as you can to the west: God is there also. The west is the place of the setting sun, and the unknown: God is still present. Whichever direction you go, God is with you (Psalm 139.8).

You may not always feel you know where you are going but you can learn to know who is with you. I often project forward 50 years. Where will I be? I do not know, but I know who I will be with, for I will be with God. God accompanies you and is ready to guide you. God will uphold you and give you courage. He will never – not ever – let you go. His hand is ready to grasp you and lead you (Psalm 139.9).

We have now looked in six directions and affirmed that God is in all of them. To these we can add, not another direction, but a new dimension, that of darkness. Darkness can come upon us in any place: even the dawn can be gloomy, cheerless and full of foreboding. In the fullness of life we can suddenly enter into darkness. Illnesses, bereavement, betrayal, loneliness, doubt and fear can all bring it about. In every life there are times when the light around us turns to night and we find ourselves groping our way forward. We may even feel Godforsaken but God never leaves us. Even if we lose our grip on God, he does not let us go and with him the night can become as clear as the day (139.10–11).

Such wonderful knowledge exceeds our intellectual understanding but it is not beyond our personal experience to feel communion with the one who knows us so well. This is a relationship of love not judgement, of liberation and support not condemnation, for God will never abandon us. The Celtic peoples often expressed this reality in prayers of encompassment for themselves and for others. Here is one such prayer from a collection gathered from the Islands and Highlands of Scotland by Alexander Carmichael in the nineteenth century. Affirm it for yourself or a loved one.

ENCOMPASSING

The compassing of God be on thee,
The compassing of the God of life.

The compassing of Christ be on thee,
The compassing of the Christ of love.

The compassing of the Spirit be on thee,
The compassing of the Spirit of Grace.

The compassing of the Three be on thee,
The compassing of the Three preserve thee,
The compassing of the Three preserve thee.
(Alexander Carmichael, *Carmina Gadelica*,
Volume III, Scottish Academic Press, 1976, p. 105)

The aim of encompassing or encircling prayers is to affirm that we are immersed in the presence of God, surrounded by him and enfolded in his love. In making such an affirmation, the Celts said they were 'making a caim'. If you wanted to do this, you would begin by facing east, raising your right hand and pointing forward. Then you would turn slowly in a sun-wise or clockwise direction until you had completed a circle. While you were doing this you could simply say 'Circle me, O God' or 'God encompasses me' or 'God is about me'. The Celts chose to go sun-wise which was called 'going deasil'; opposite to this is widdershins which was going against the clock and the way of the world. The Celts warned if you went against the way of the world too often something terrible was likely to happen to you. This in itself is acting out a truth: we cannot be seeking help from God if we are going against nature.

I can still remember when I was 11 and in a woodwork class. I was having some difficulty with my project and took a plane apart three times to sharpen the blade. Yet when I used it, I was still roughing up the wood. The lesson was almost at an end when the teacher came and said, 'It's no use sharpening the blade if you will continue to go against the grain!' There is a lesson for life here. If you go against the grain in nature you should expect life to be rough.

When Celtic people met trouble or evil, they would draw the caim around themselves as a person would pull a cloak about them in a storm. Because we are not almighty, we need to call upon the Almighty. Rather than opting out, running away or wallowing in our troubles, we can turn to the one who gives us the power to live life in all its fullness. When we cannot lift ourselves up or pull ourselves together, help is at hand from the Lord who made heaven and earth. Why exhaust ourselves by going on alone when we can rest and acknowledge that God is all too ready to aid us? Rather than revealing our weakness, putting our faith in him gives us the courage to stand and to withstand all kinds of troubles – along with the assurance to be ourselves in the midst of these – for we know we are no longer operating in our strength alone.

Many of the saints have expressed the encompassing of God. In the fourth century, in his 'Treatise on the Trinity', Hilary of Poitiers wrote:

> I came to see that there is no space without God: space does not exist apart from God. God is in heaven, in hell and beyond the seas. God lives in everything and enfolds everything. God embraces all that is, and is embraced by the universe: confined to no part within it he encompasses all that exists.
>
> (Quoted in Robert Atwell, *Celebrating the Saints*,
> SCM Press, 2004, p. 37)

Julian of Norwich, in the fourteenth century, more than once expressed we are 'wrapped around and enfolded in God':

> He is our clothing. In his love he wraps and holds us. He enfolds us for love, and he will never let us go.
>
> (Julian of Norwich, *Enfolded in Love*,
> Darton, Longman and Todd, 1980, p. 1)

And again she said:

> As the body is clad in clothes, and the flesh in skin, and the bones in flesh, and the heart in the whole, so are we clothed, body and soul, in the goodness of God and enfolded in it.
>
> (Julian of Norwich, *Enfolded in Love*, p. 6)

In the twentieth century, Teilhard de Chardin expressed the same encompassing in his phrase *Le Milieu divin*, which is the title of one of his most famous books:

God who made man that he might seek him – God whom we try to apprehend by the groping of our lives – that self-same God is as pervasive and perceptible as the atmosphere in which we are bathed. He encompasses us on all sides, like the world itself. What prevents you, then, from enfolding him in your arms? Only one thing: your inability to see him ... The true God, the Christian God, will under your gaze, invade the universe ... He will penetrate it as a ray of light does a crystal ... God truly waits for us in things, unless indeed he advances to meet us.

> (Pierre Teilhard de Chardin, *Le Milieu divin*,
> Collins Fontana, 1975, pp. 46–7)

This same encompassing is expressed in many hymns. I like this one in particular:

> In heav'nly love abiding,
> no change my heart shall fear;
> and safe is such confiding,
> for nothing changes here:
> the storm may roar without me,
> my heart may low be laid;
> but God is round about me
> and can I be dismayed?
> (Anna Laetitia Waring, 1820–1910)

When I first sang these words it was with a great sense of opting out, for I imagined they were about when we die and are in heaven! But, in fact, this heavenly love is being sung of by someone who is rejoicing in the love and power of God *now*, while struggling with the ways of the world. At this very moment, we can rejoice in God's love and know that we not only abide in his love but in his kingdom, which is the kingdom of heaven.

In the next chapter, we will explore 'The prayer of seven directions'. But first, you might like to affirm the encompassing of God in these words of mine. Spend time with them until you can personally say with some assurance, 'In him we live and move and have our being' (Acts 17.28).

> Circle me, O God
> Keep hope within
> Despair without.
>
> Circle me, O God,
> Keep peace within
> Keep turmoil out.
>
> Circle me, O God,
> Keep calm within
> Keep storms without.
>
> Circle me, O God,
> Keep strength within
> Keep weakness out.
> (David Adam, *The Edge of Glory*,
> Triangle/SPCK, 1985,
> p. 8, adapted)

The prayer of seven directions

Christ as a light,
Illumine and guide me!
Christ as a shield o'er shadow and cover me!
Christ be under me! Christ be over me!
Christ be beside me,
On left hand and right!
Christ be before me, behind me, about me!
Christ this day, be within and without me!

This is part of James Clarence Mangan's translation of 'St Patrick's Breastplate' and it first appeared in *Duffy's Magazine*. It was later printed in Mangan's *Collected Poems* (New York, 1859).

I have often taught the content of this prayer to individuals and to groups of people – schoolchildren as well as adults. When I tell youngsters they are to learn, act out and dance 'The prayer of seven directions', they enjoy the idea that prayer can be expressed not only in words but also in movement. We explore the directions of up and down, before us, behind us, on our right and on our left. We all agree it is easy to learn these but then someone will inevitably say, 'That's only six directions.' I'll tell them they have to absorb these before we move on to the seventh direction. Looking at the prayer, many will spot that this is 'God within me'. I'll ask if anyone has really experienced God within and suggest it is better to learn we are in God's presence before discovering that he is also in us.

I tend to put the directions in the order that flows best if they are being acted out as an encompassing prayer (see below).

I sometimes encourage people to have 'God' as the subject of the prayer, though it is fine to use 'Christ' or 'The Father' or 'The Holy Spirit', and I like to change 'be' to 'is' to reflect that we are not making a request but opening our lives to the reality that we are not alone. You may like to take your time to affirm the seven directions and to rejoice in the reality of what you are saying:

> God is before me,
> God on my right,
> God is behind me,
> God on my left,
> God is beneath me,
> God is above me
> God is within me.

Whenever possible, I encourage groups to meet in a circle. As we all face each direction in turn, I stress that we are not making God come to us, but rather opening our lives to God, who is always with us.

Sometimes I tell people about the words of the Indian poet Kabir that are written on a fountain in India:

I laugh when I hear that the fish in the sea are thirsty:
I laugh when I hear man goes in search of God.

I'll ask why the poet thinks it is funny that people go in search of God, as this is a good way of prompting everyone to explore the reality that God *is* with us and that we live *in* him.

With adult groups, I often read the words from Francis Thompson's poem 'The Kingdom of God':

O world invisible, we view thee
O world intangible, we touch thee,
O world unknowable, we know thee,
Inapprehensible, we clutch thee!
Does the fish soar to find the ocean,
The eagle plunge to find the air –
That we ask of the stars in motion
If they have rumour of thee there?
Not where the wheeling systems darken,
And our benumbed conceiving soars! –
The drift of pinions, would we hearken,
Beats at our own clay-shuttered doors.
The angels keep their ancient places –
Turn but a stone and start a wing!
'Tis ye, 'tis your estrangèd faces,
That miss the many-splendoured thing.
(*Selected Poems of Francis Thompson*,
Methuen/Burns & Oates, 1909,
pp. 132–3)

It is all too easy to 'shutter our doors' to God and we need to learn how to open them again and to increase our awareness of his abiding with us and within us. The prayer of seven directions helps us to turn to him and call upon his love and his aid – to immerse ourselves in the great reality that God *is* with us.

Now let us work our way through the seven directions. You may like to begin by facing east, the place of the rising sun and the start of the day.

'God is before me'

It is important to get beginnings right as then we shall be less likely to fail to do what we aim to. So let's affirm that we are not alone: our God is with us. At the beginning of life, at the beginning of each minute, at the beginning of any new event – wherever we go, whatever we do – God is there. We may not know what lies ahead, but we know God waits for us and seeks to meet us in everything. Give yourself in love to him who gives himself to you. Affirm now that God is before you. Say to yourself in each happening of the day, 'God is here, his Spirit is with me.'

'God on my right'

Turn to the south, the direction of the midday sun. In the fullness of the day, and the busyness and business of life, it is too easy to forget the Lord is there in our midst.

God, the giver of life, is in the very thick of things. He is with you when things are hectic, so find peace in the midst of activity by learning to turn to him. God is present in the fullness of life, when you are using your skills to the utmost and operating at the peak of your abilities. God is with you in all you seek to do or achieve. In him you can find strength and courage. Rejoice that he is with you and ask him for his peace and power in the midst of your daily living. If you are meeting as a group in a circle, take hold of the hand of the person on your right and know that God meets both of you in the other. Say to them: 'The Lord is with you.'

You may like to teach yourself to say in the busyness of life or near midday, 'God is here, his Spirit is with me.'

'God is behind me'

Turn now to the west, to where the sun goes down. God is there behind you to protect you from your own past and from all that would assail your mind and spirit in the dark. He is there when you discover your frailty or sin. He is with you in the dark places of memory. He comes offering forgiveness and seeks to give you rest and peace so you may be renewed in him. He is with you on the sunset road, often unnoticed but always there; he abides with you. When powers wane and the lights go dim he is still there. Though you cannot see him he is still with you. When the way seems dark, when you are troubled in mind, or when strength is failing, you are not alone: affirm, 'God is here, his Spirit is with me.'

'God on my left'

Turn to the north where the sun does not reach. This is the place of darkness and the unknown. But the darkness is no threat to God. God is present in our darkness and in the darkness of the world. When sinister things are happening to you and in the world around you, God never leaves you. It is often at this moment you know you need a power and a light that is not of your making. It is when you face darkness within or around yourself that you know you need the power of God, the Saviour. You need him who created light out of darkness and him who is the Light of the World. In his strength alone you can face the last great darkness of death. When you find you are in the dark it is good to affirm, 'God is here, his Spirit is with me', or to say, 'Jesus Christ is the Light of the World: a Light that no darkness can extinguish.' If you are meeting in a circle, take the hand of the person on your left and know that God is to be met in them. Say, 'The Lord is with you.' When night closes around you affirm, 'God is here, his Spirit is with me.'

'God is beneath me'

At this point you can look down or touch the ground. Earth your prayers by remembering that you are of the dust of the earth and only in the love of God can you hope for life eternal. God beneath you is ready to uphold you and to bear you up.

Know that 'underneath are the everlasting arms' (Deuteronomy 33.27, KJV). However deep you sink you will discover God is there: 'if I make the grave my bed, you are there also'. In times of trouble or when weakness comes, let his strength bear you up. God in Christ was found in all the depths of life; he descended into all the hells of this world and even to death. If you look at the hands that support you, you will see they are hands of love that bear the imprint of the nails of the cross. Know you are in the hands of God. When you stumble or fall or when you are feeling down, know that God seeks to sustain and raise you up. Our God is the God of the resurrection and newness of life. Rejoice in the resurrection of our Lord from the darkness of the tomb and say, 'In you, O Christ, I arise. Alleluia.' Whenever life seems dismal and you feel down, affirm, 'God is here, his Spirit is with me.'

'God is above me'

Raise your sights and look up. Stretch up high with arms slightly apart. Know that though God is higher than your thoughts, he can be reached by love. Stretch your whole being in love, and grasp for the love of God. Be uplifted by the knowledge that God is not far off and that he loves you. In Christ, God who descended to the earth also ascended into heaven. He came down with a purpose, to raise you up. He died that you might live and have life in all its fullness. He entered the grave that you might arise to the fullness of eternal life. He became human that you might share in the divine. This is not just for a future life, it is for now: lift up your heart and rejoice. Rejoice in your salvation. Rejoice that life is eternal and nothing can separate you from the love of God. You may like to say, 'In him I arise and in him I live and move and have my being.' In times of joy and wonder, with your eyes, hands, heart and mind raised, affirm, 'God is here, his Spirit is with me.'

You have now completed six directions, which is as much as the psalmist did in Psalm 139. As a result you can say, 'I am encompassed by God' or 'God is all around me'. You can utter to God in love, 'You encircle me, O God.' Once you have expressed that God is all around you and that God is far greater than you are or can even imagine, then you are ready to affirm the seventh direction. Conscious that you are in God, in his love and goodness, you can move on to say:

'God is within me'

Raise your hands and with your fingers point to the centre of your chest and say 'God is within me'. It is not that you possess God: God is not an object to be owned. Rather, his Spirit permeates your whole life. Like the air you breathe, God is all around you and within you. You may like to breathe gently a few times and with each intake of breath say, 'God is with me and within me.' God and you are in common union, in communion with each other. You do not need to travel to find God, for he is with you and about you and within. Rejoice that you dwell in God and God is in you. You may like to say, 'God, I live in you and you live in me.' Rest in his presence and enjoy his love for you. Affirm, 'God is here, his Spirit is with me and within me.'

You have completed the seven directions. It is good to affirm them once more; you may like to act these out as you do so:

> God is before me,
> God on my right,
> God is behind me,
> God on my left,
> God is beneath me,
> God is above me
> God is within me.

At some stage, move from affirmation to personal prayer, speaking directly to God with simplicity and saying:

> God, you are before me.
> God, you are on my right.
> God, you are behind me.
> God, you are on my left.
> God, you are beneath me.
> God, you are above me.
> God, you are within me.

Make yourself familiar with this pattern and make the prayer of seven directions your own.

In order to help you discover how rich the seven directions are in content, each of the following chapters provides prayers for one direction, to guide you into your own prayers. The seven directions help us understand that the gift of God's presence to us is not exclusive; God's love is not for us alone. He gives himself in love to all of his creation and asks us to do the same. Just as you may have held hands with the person on your right and left, this is part of the great adventure of seeing God in everyone you meet. Sometimes he comes in the most impenetrable of disguises: sometimes his presence is so marred or covered over that you may find it hard to discern. But God is in everyone and wants you to encounter him there. Gandhi once said, 'If you don't find God in the next person you meet, it is a waste of time looking for him further.' It was after a visit to our home by a tramp that I wrote the following:

> You are the caller
> You are the poor
> You are the stranger at my door
>
> You are the wanderer
> The unfed

> You are the homeless
> With no bed
>
> You are the man
> Driven insane
> You are the child
> Crying in pain
>
> You are the other who comes to me
> If I open to another you're born in me.
> (David Adam, *The Edge of*
> *Glory*, p. 34)

We are called to see Christ in others, and to be Christ to others. We are given the opportunity to let God work within us and through us. We are asked to be aware of and to respect God in our fellow beings. The words that the angel said to Mary at the Annunciation should echo in our hearts whoever we meet: 'Dominus tecum', 'The Lord *is* with you' (Luke 1.28, my italics). Seek to discover that God comes to you and speaks to you through other people. God's love is revealed in the love we have for one another. The encompassing of God touches everyone: we all dwell in him and he in us. Rejoice that you meet God in others.

Another extension of 'The prayer of seven directions' is to realize that God created the world and that he loves it dearly. We cannot truly say we are devoted to God if we destroy his creation – the world he has given to us and in which he wants us to encounter his presence and love. If we open our eyes, we will discover that even the smallest thing has the potential to create wonder and awe – to be a stepping stone into the great unknown; to lead us into a deep sense of mystery. I thrill each time I read these words from *Le Milieu divin*:

We have only to go a little beyond the frontier of sensible appearances in order to see the divine welling up and showing through. But it is not only close to us, in front of us, that the divine presence has revealed itself. It has sprung up universally, and we find ourselves so surrounded and transfixed by it, that there is no room left to fall down and adore it, even within ourselves.

By means of all created things, without exception, the divine assails us, penetrates us and moulds us. We imagined it as distant and inaccessible, whereas in fact we live steeped in its burning layers. *In eo vivimus.*

(Teilhard de Chardin, *Le Milieu divin*, p. 112)

I feel the same when I read Gerard Manley Hopkins' poem 'God's Grandeur' saying:

> The world is charged with the grandeur of God.
> It will flame out, like shining from shook foil

The early Celtic Christians were often accused of being pan-theists because of their joyous expression of God in all things. You could of course ask, if God is not in all things, is he anywhere on earth? The Celtic Christians are actually better regarded as pan-en-theists who saw all in God and God in all. They recognized that the mysterious, the transcendent, is to be found among us. When we are truly aware of the wonders of the world we should, in awe, rejoice and give thanks that we are part of a wonderful creation. We can say with George Herbert (1593–1633):

> Teach me, my God and King,
> in all things Thee to see

The God who encompasses us encompasses all things. You may like to meditate on the piece below before you move onto the prayers in the chapters following:

> He, who created you,
> Calls you to awaken
> To his presence
> Around you and within you.
> The same presence
> Is to be found
> In all of creation,
> In every blade of grass,
> In the sun that shines,
> In the winds that blow,
> In the dust of the earth,
> In the shimmering sea
> In everyone you meet.
> He is in all there is,
> He fills all,
> And yet is beyond all.
> Do not detach yourself
> From the earth
> Seek to love it
> As God loves it.
> He is to be found here
> In this world
> And in this moment

GOD IN THE BEGINNING

GOD, IN YOU, I ARISE

God, I arise today in your presence
You encircle me with your power
You enfold me in your peace

God, I arise today in your strength
You are my shield and support
You are my salvation and song

God, I arise today in your love
You bestow on me your light
You fill my heart with longing

God, I arise today by your grace
You give me of your goodness
You provide me with your guiding
God, in you, I arise

BEGINNING IN GOD

God, in the beginning of creation
God, in the beginning of space
God, in the beginning of time
God in my life

God, in the beginning of existence
God, in the beginning of humankind
God, in the beginning of each breath
God in my life

God, in the beginning of the year
God, in the beginning of each hour
God, in the beginning of every second
God in my life

God, in the beginning of each thought
God, in the beginning of every word
God, in the beginning of each deed
God in my life

God, in each beginning
God, here and with me now
God, in this day to its close and for ever
God in my life

THE GIFT

God, as I rejoice in the gift of this new day,
Teach me to unwrap it gently and without haste.
There may be much that is fragile within it,
Things that could be lost if I am not careful.
Help me to enjoy the unwrapping,
And to delight in the present given to me.
Let me discern within that gift your love:
Your generosity and grace towards me.
But above all help me be aware of you:
For in the giving of the present you also give
    yourself.
Let me not be forever seeking gifts from you,
But rejoicing in getting to know you,
And learning more of your great love for me,
For the greatest present in the present is your
    presence.

DEDICATING THE DAY

Lord, as I begin this new day,
Give me a glimpse of your glory.
Strengthen my relationship with you
And enkindle the flame of my love.
Clear away what mists my vision,
Tune my mind to the wonders about me,
And teach me to be grateful for your mercies.

Make me aware that I always live in you
And help me abide in awe and adoration.
Open my ears to your call in the needy;
Open my eyes to see you in others;
Open my lips to proclaim your praise;
Strengthen my hands to do your will;
Guide my steps in every journey I take,
And give me a heart that throbs with your love.

God, make me aware of you in all that I do.

GLORY TO YOU, O LORD

For the miracle of the universe
From the nebulae to the neutron
From the macrocosm to the microcosm
Glory to you, O Lord

For the birth of our planet
The seas, the sky, the earth
For sun, moon and light
Glory to you, O Lord

For the wonder of life itself
For every living creature
For the powers you give to me
Glory to you, O Lord

For your presence in all
For your power through all
For your abiding with all
Glory to you, O Lord

LORD, OPEN MY LIFE

Lord, widen my vision
That I may know you
In your creation
And through your creation.
Though you are greater
Than all things and not bound by them,
You can be found within all
By those who have eyes to see.
May I perceive all life as holy
And all places as sacred:
For you have made all out of your love
And for your love.
Touch my heart
That I may respect all things
And honour all people:
For you dwell in them
And they dwell in you.
Lord, open my life
To your glory this day.

AWAKENING

God, in your presence, I awake.
You are here at this day's dawning,
As night shadows creep away
And the time comes for arising.
God, in you I rejoice.

God, in your light I awake.
You illuminate my way:
All may not be well within me,
But your brightness cheers my day.
God, in you I rejoice.

God, in your love I awake.
You hold me in your heart.
I feel myself drawn into you,
And know you will never depart.
God, in you I rejoice.

God, in your grace, I awake.
This life is a gift; I cannot earn it;
You shower me with your glory
And help me to live it.
God, in you I rejoice.

God, in you, I awake.
You are about me and at my side.
My very being depends on you.
Help me know this and to abide.
God, in you I rejoice.

LORD, OPEN MY EYES

Lord, open my eyes to the newness of this day
Lord, open my eyes, clouded with night
Lord, open my eyes, misted with prejudice
Lord, open my eyes, blinded to beauty
Lord, open my eyes, dimmed with sorrow
Lord, open my eyes, closed through fear
Lord, open my eyes and make me aware
Lord, open my eyes to be more sensitive
Lord, open my eyes and increase my appreciation
Lord, open my eyes to a vision of your glory
Lord, open my eyes to your presence with me

GOD, I REJOICE IN YOU

God, I am in your presence.
You are here at the dawning
Of each perfect new day.
You are with me always:
God, I rejoice in you.

God, I am in your loving care.
You enfold me in your being,
And hold me safe in your heart.
You are with me always:
God, I rejoice in you.

God, I am in your light.
Though the darkness is near,
You illumine my way.
You are with me always:
God, I rejoice in you.

God, I am in your grace.
You surround me with glory,
You touch me with your greatness.
You are with me always:
God, I rejoice in you.

I COMMIT MYSELF TO YOU

God, I commit myself to your keeping
This day to your protection
My plans to your direction
My busyness to your stillness
My heart to your love
My troubles to your peace

God ever with me
Be my wisdom in my thinking
Be my guide in my actions
Be my love in my dealings
Be my life in my whole being
Be my strength in times of weakness
Be my shield when troubles assail
Be my song and salvation now and for ever

GOD IN THE MIDST OF LIFE

YOU ARE WITH ME

Lord, wherever I go today
Your love encompasses me
Your peace enfolds me
Your hand protects me
Your eye beholds me
Your power strengthens me
Your grace goes with me

Lord, open my eyes
And make me mindful
That in the midst of life
You are always there
And that whatever happens today
You will be with me on the way

DEDICATION

Lord, as I set out today
Make me aware of your glory
Open my eyes to your presence

In the many events of the day
Prompt me to be attentive
And to heed you calling me

In my encounters with others
Help me to know your love
And to show your love

In each passing hour
Give me time for wonder
A stillness to know you
And the power of your presence

Lord, grant that I may live to your glory

GOD WITH US

Lord, you are present
And at work in your world.
I need you to open my eyes
To the glory of your presence:
To stir my mind to your grace.
Then, take my hands
And work through me.
Touch my mouth
And speak though me.
Warm my heart
And love through me.
Lord, as you abide in us,
May we reveal you to others
And see you in others.

LORD, TEACH ME TO LOVE

Lord, teach me to pray
To pray is to love you
To love you is to give myself
To give myself fully to you
To love you with all my heart

Lord, to love you
Is to give my love to the world
With the love you have for it
To love each leaf, each flower
Each animal, each creature
To respect the earth and all in it

Lord, to love you
Is to love others as you love them
To reach out to friend and stranger
To care for the poor and oppressed
To forgive and to have compassion
To accept people as they are

Lord to love you
Is to learn to love myself
With the love that you have for me
To rejoice in my being
To reach out in love beyond myself
To the world, to others, to you

Lord, teach us to love one another
As you love us

FIRE OF LOVE

Fire of love
Kindle my heart
Set me ablaze with love
For you, O God
For the world
For my home
For my neighbour
For myself
Let love be in
My speaking
My thinking
My actions
Today
Tomorrow
For ever

IN THE BUSYNESS OF LIFE

Lord, in the busyness of life
Keep me close to you.
Grant me a sense of wonder,
An attitude of reverence,
A deep feeling of awe,
An awareness of your presence.
Enfold me in your peace:
Encompass me with your protection

Lord, give me the sense to seek you,
The stillness to make room for you,
The sensitivity to be aware of you,
A mind that is receptive to you,
A heart that burns with love for you.
Strengthen my relationship with you
That I may rejoice in you all this day.

GOD IN ALL

God,
In all our possibilities and potential,
In our plans and our purpose,
In our promises and pleasures,
In our problems and perplexities,
In our play and in our pastimes,
In our pains and in our perils,
In our powers and in our passions,
Of your presence and your peace,
You provide us.

THE COMING OF THE LORD

Wisdom of God, fill my mind
With an awareness of your presence.
Root of Jesse, teach me
To respect my home and loved ones.
Key of David, open to me
The way that leads to the fullness of life.
Morning Star, deliver me from darkness
And help me walk in the light of your love.
King of the Gentiles, teach me to love all
With the love that you have for them.
Emmanuel, Lord, you are here with me
In times of work and rest, in joy and sorrow.
Light of the World, scatter all dullness
With the glory of your presence.
Christ, you are come to dwell with me:
Help me to abide with and in you
In the busyness of this day and always.

GOD, YOU COME TO ME

God you come! You come to me! You come to my aid.
Your presence is all around me:
In your presence is peace.

God you come! You come to me! You come to my
home.
Your presence is all around me:
In your presence is love.

God you come! You come to me! You come to my
working.
Your presence is all around me:
In your presence is strength.

God you come! You come to me! You come to my
journeying.
God, you abide with me and in me:
In your presence is courage.

God you come! You come to me!
Teach me to abide in you:
In your presence is life and life eternal.

GOD, ENCIRCLING ME

God, encircling me,
God in my life,
God in my waking,
God in my travelling,
God in my working,
God in my busyness,
God in my activities
God in my achieving,
God in my resting,
God in my sleeping,
God in my rejoicing,
God in my sorrowing,
God deep in my heart
God in my life.

GOD IN ALL THAT HAS BEEN

LET ME REST IN YOU

Lord, I have raced through this day
Forgive me when I have ignored you
The times I have been unaware of your glory
When my eyes have been blind to your beauty
When my ears have been deaf to your call
The times I have been insensitive to wonder
When my heart has been hard and cold
When my mind was too preoccupied

Still me, Lord, and teach me to love
Still my restless being with your peace
Still me in body, mind and spirit
Let me rest in you and in your power
As the darkness comes, heal me
Transfigure me with your glory.

IN YOU I AM MADE WHOLE

Lord, I feel wrung out and drained:
I come to your fullness for renewal.
Lord, I am weary, worn and woeful:
I come to you for your power.

Lord, I am lethargic, lonely and lost:
I come to rejoice in your presence.
Lord, above all, I come not for gifts:
But to give you myself in love.

Lord, in you is life and life eternal:
In you I am made whole.

IN GOD

As evening draws on
I seek the peace of God
In him is perfect rest

As the darkness descends
I seek the love of the Saviour
In him is the resurrection

As the night approaches
I seek the power of the Spirit
In him is the breath of life

As the daylight fades
I seek the company of the Trinity
The protection of the Holy Three

MY LIGHT AND MY SALVATION

Lord, you are my light and my salvation
You walk with me in the hidden places of my life
The dark places where I am afraid to walk alone
Where I need the light of your presence and love

Lord, you are my light and my salvation
You walk with me in the hidden rooms of shame
Where I need your forgiveness and renewal

Lord, you are my light and my salvation
You walk with me in the troubled depth of my being
Where I need your peaceful presence and calm

Lord, you are my light and my salvation
You walk with me in my store of hurtful memories
Bringing your healing and renewal

Lord, you are my light and my salvation
You walk with me and accept me as I am
You cleanse me from my secret faults
Forgive me and give me life anew

Lord, I rejoice in you and your saving power
Lord, you are my light and my salvation

AT PEACE

God, I am at peace
Because you enfold me
I come now to rest
In your protecting
Nothing can separate us
I know that you love me
And that changes everything
In your presence, troubles fade
And all anxieties decrease
I dwell in you and you in me
I am already in your kingdom

SURROUND ME, O GOD

When life is hard
And strength is gone
When fears descend
And I cannot go on
Encircle me, O God
In your great might
Deliver me, O God
From the dark night
Surround me, O God
Now and each hour
Save me, O God
Keep me in your power
Strengthen me, O God
By the might of your arm
Hold me close, O God
Protect me from harm

AS DARKNESS DESCENDS

God, as darkness descends
Open my eyes to your presence:
You are my light and my love,
You are my strength and my salvation
And the darkness is no darkness with you.

Holy God, Holy and Strong One,
Stand between me and every darkness.
Bountiful God, ever gracious and giving,
Stand between me and each emptiness.
Loving God and enfolding God,
Stand between me and each heartache.
Ever-present God and abiding,
Stand between me and each loneliness.
Almighty and powerful God,
Stand between me and each weakness.
Holy God, Holy and Strong One,
You are with me now and always.

GRANT ME YOUR PEACE, LORD

God, the day's events have been disturbing
Many troubles are distressing me
I am not at rest or at ease
Grant me your peace, Lord

I am not calm in myself
I am not in harmony with others
I feel there is war within me
Grant me your peace, Lord

God, I need to find rest in you
Show me the way that leads to tranquillity
Help me to accept your serenity
Grant me your peace, Lord

God, save me from the easy peace I should avoid
And direct me to the kind I should share and
   work for
Peace I should gratefully receive
Grant me your peace, Lord

God, in you alone is my peace
The peace which the world cannot give
The peace which passes all understanding
Grant me your peace, Lord

ENFOLD ME, LORD

God of all power and might
Enfold me, Lord, in your light
When I am tempted to despair
Enfold me, Lord, in your care
When troubles come and assail my soul
Enfold me, Lord, keep me whole
When I am in mortal agony
Enfold me, Lord, set me free
When lonely, alone or full of fear
Enfold me, Lord, for you are near
When I am about to die
Enfold me, Lord, raise me high

OUT OF OUR DARKNESS

From despair and depression
From darkness and drabness
From dullness and desperation
Lord of light, deliver us

From vandalism and violence
From crassness and carelessness
From insensitivity and idleness
Lord of light, deliver us

From hardness and hatred
From baseness and blindness
From coldness and callousness
Lord of light, deliver us

From greed and gracelessness,
From selfishness and sinfulness
From indifference and ignorance
Lord of light, deliver us

PRESENCE EVER NEAR

The God of light is round me
The dark I need not fear
The light of God is with me
His presence ever near

God's grace abounds to guide me
His goodness also here
The grace of God is with me
His presence ever near

God's power is all about me
His peace is also here
The power of God is with me
His presence ever near

God in love enfolds me
His kindness gives me cheer
The love of God is with me
His presence ever near

HAVE MERCY ON US

Lord, have mercy on us
Protect us through this night
Lord, have mercy on us
Surround us with your light

Christ, have mercy on us
From our sins set free
Christ, have mercy on us
Let us find our rest in thee

Spirit, have mercy on us
Circle us with your power
Spirit, have mercy on us
Guide us in this hour

THOUGH THE NIGHT COMES

Though the night comes
And darkness is about me
Help me to see
Your presence and mystery

Though the night comes
And I enter the unknown
Help me to know
I am not on my own

Though the night comes
And the evening is drear
Grant me your light
And make me aware

Though the night comes
And I am full of alarm
Encompass me, God
Keep me from harm

Though the night comes
And I face the end
The darkness is scattered
For you are my friend

Though the night comes
And I am distressed
Come Lord of grace
Grant me your rest

LORD, LET YOUR LIGHT SHINE

Lord, your light pierces the darkness
Within me and about me
In your grace and glory
You never leave me
Let your light shine in the dark places
In the hidden and painful memories
In my sorrows and past sins
In the depth of my being
Bring me out of darkness
And into your glorious light
Forgive, redeem, restore me
Give me a clean heart, O God
Renew a right spirit within me

GOD IN THE END OF
ALL THINGS

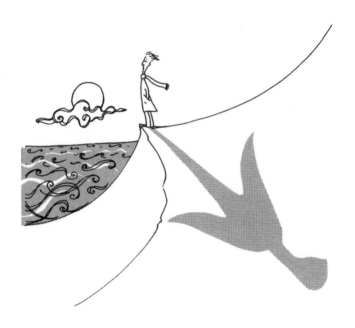

GOD IN THE NIGHT

Father of all creation
Maker of the world
Holy and Strong One
Encircling all there is
Around me this night

Christ, Saviour of us all
Redeemer of the world
Holy and Strong One
Encircling all there is
Around me this night

Spirit, breath of life
Inspiring and guiding
Holy and Strong One
Encircling all there is
Around me this night

Holy and blessed Three
Glorious Trinity
Three persons in unity
Encircling all there is
Around me this night

THE NIGHT IS YOURS

Lord God, the day is yours
The night is yours
With you the night
Is as clear as the day
You walk in the darkness
And turn the shadow of death
Into a new morning
Lord, shine in my heart
Like the sunrise
Disperse the darkness
Of doubt and despair
So when the new day dawns
I may arise in your presence
In your love and in your glory

DARKNESS IS ABOUT ME

Lord, the darkness is about me
I need the light of your presence
I feel empty and heavy-hearted
I need to be uplifted by your power
I find myself indifferent and cold
I need the warmth of your love

Lord, I am weary and troubled
I need to rest and be at peace in you
Lord, above all things I long for you
To teach me the way of stillness
Lord, lead me into silence
That I may hear you and abide with you

RENEW ME, LORD

Lord, renew my strength
Wipe out my sin with your forgiveness
Transform my weakness with your power
Deliver me from terror and all fear of the night

Into my weariness breathe your life
Into my darkness bring your light
Into my loneliness bring your presence
Let me know you abide with me tonight

LORD, IN YOU I TRUST

Lord, in the darkness
Be there as my light
Lord, in my weakness
Hold me in your strength

Lord, be my defence
Be my shield
Be my protection
Lord, be my Saviour and deliverer

Lord, in you I hope
Lord, in you I trust
Lord, in you alone
Is life eternal

SCATTER THE DARKNESS

Come, Lord, scatter the darkness within
Disperse the clouds of fear with your brightness
Dispel the mists of doubt with your radiance
Destroy the gloom of my mind with your shining
And let the light of your countenance enlighten me

NIGHT PRAYER

God of power and might
Be known to me this night
God of power and might
Surround me with your light
God of power and might
Be with me in my plight
God of power and might
Protect me from any slight
God of power and might
Save me from all fright
God of power and might
Help me evil fight
God of power and might
In you let me delight
God of power and might
Be known to me this night

NINEFOLD KYRIES

I who am your child
Call upon you, O Father
Lord, have mercy
I who am weary
Call upon you, giver of life
Lord, have mercy
I who am mortal
Call upon you, Immortal One
Lord, have mercy

I who feel lost
Call upon you, Good Shepherd
Christ, have mercy
I who am sinful
Call upon you, my Saviour
Christ, have mercy
I who am down
Call upon you, Risen One
Christ, have mercy

I who am dispirited
Call upon you, Breath of Life
Lord, have mercy
I who am feeling worn
Call upon you, Life-giving Spirit
Lord, have mercy
I who have gone astray
Call upon you, my Lord and Guide
Lord, have mercy

COME, MY LOVE

Lord, I open myself to your presence:
Let your love so fill my darkness
That it blazes with your glory.
Lord, replace my feeling of emptiness
With the assurance of your presence.
Bring your joy to my distress;
Bring your peace to my troubles;
Bring your hope to my fears;
Bring your strength to my weakness;
Bring your love to my loneliness.
Lord, I open my whole being to you,
Knowing you give yourself to me.

LIGHT OF THE WORLD

Light of the World, you are here in my darkness,
Guiding, protecting, defending me from all evil.
You stand between me and all that seeks to darken
    my life.
Come now into my past with your forgiveness and
    peace.
Shine in the dark and hidden places, in the secret
    rooms of sin
And disperse my deep regrets and sorrow.
Chase away my fears and calm my inmost anxieties,
    Lord Christ,
For I trust and put my hope in you.
Redeem me, renew me and restore me,
That I may walk in your light
And in the fullness of life which is eternal.

BE MY LIGHT THIS NIGHT

Creator of the light
Maker of sun, moon and stars
Giving brightness to the world
Be my light this night

Christ, Light of the World
Conquering over death
Giving new hope to the world
Be my light this night

Spirit, descending as fire
Guiding and inspiring
Giving wisdom to the world
Be my light this night

Creator of light
Christ the light
Spirit of Light
Be my light this night

HOLY AND MERCIFUL

God of the darkness
Bringer of night
Father of glory
Grant me your light

Christ my Saviour
Cleansing from sin
Christ my redeemer
Grant peace within

Spirit all-powerful
By you I am blest
Spirit of renewal
Grant to me rest

Holy and Merciful
Almighty Three
With me tonight
Be protecting me

GOD ABOVE ALL

LORD, BEYOND IN OUR MIDST

Lord, you are the beyond in our midst
Your kingdom is not far off
It is here and always at hand
Though we cannot see you
We can enjoy your presence
And enter into your kingdom
You reveal your nearness
In the beauty around us
In the sunlight and the stars
In the mighty sea and quiet earth
You can be discovered
In the smallest flower
In the trees of the wood
Yet you are always beyond them
Lord, give us grace to see
With eyes cleansed
That all can be transfigured
And reveal your glory

REVEALED IN LOVE

Lord, you are beyond all images.
How can I know you, but through love?
Without your love for us,
We could not reach you.
Unless you love us,
We cannot approach you.
But that you come to us,
We could never find you.
It is in knowing that you love us
That we can dare to love you.
Because your love is
For all of your creation,
When we love the world,
We share in your love for it
And we are one with you.

When we love our neighbour,
With acceptance and forgiveness,
You reveal your love in us.
You are not far from any of us.
And when we love ourselves,
With the love you have for us,
Then we can say we know you,
Even though you are beyond us,
For you are in our midst.

THOUGH I CANNOT SEE YOU

Lord, though I cannot see you,
You reveal yourself in the love
Of my family and my friends.
You warm my heart by your presence.

Lord, though I cannot see you,
You show yourself through creation,
In the mystery and otherness of things.
You inspire in me wonder and awe.

Lord, though I cannot see you,
You speak to me in times of stillness:
In the calm of your presence is peace.
You protect me from all harm.

Lord, though I cannot see you,
You never leave me on my own:
You surround me in loving power.
You are there when I am in danger.

Lord, though I cannot see you,
You are the God above:
You are with and around me,
You enfold me in your love.

BE STILL AND KNOW

To pray you need silence
Silence before prayer
Silence during prayer
Silence after prayer
Silence that is attentive
Silence between words
Silence that is loving
Silence that reaches out
Silence of the mind
Silence in wonder
Silence in communion

God, teach me to be silent
Silent before your mystery
Silent before the other
Silent at home with self
With a silence opening my life
Not talking about silence
But living and breathing silence
Let silence fill my days
Let your silence change my life

ENLARGE MY HEART

Love without beginning
And without end
Ever-faithful one
Hidden mystery
Beyond all imagining
Reality beyond words
Presence beyond understanding
Unseen yet ever near

Touch my heart
That I may know love is your meaning
That before I knew you
You have loved me
And that love never ceases
Enlarge my heart
So that I can comprehend you
In love

LORD, WE NEED TO KNOW YOU

Lord unseen, we need to know you.
Without you life has no lasting meaning;
Without you we move towards nothing;
Without you we live in darkness;
Without you only death is certain.
But with you is life and purpose;
With you is the gift of love;
With you alone is life eternal.
Help us, Lord, to truly know you,
To rejoice in your presence,
To seek to do your will,
And to love you with our whole being
As you love us, Lord God.

WONDERFUL GOD

Wonderful love
Wonderful God
You made me
You are with me
Wonderful God

You behold me
You enfold me
You sought me
You bought me
Wonderful God

You are above me
You are beneath me
You are with me
You are within me
Wonderful God

You are before me
You are behind me
You ever love me
You never leave me
Wonderful God

You are at my right
You are at my left
You encircle me
You surround me
Wonderful God

GOD BEYOND IMAGES

God, your presence is beyond our imagining
Your love is greater than our hearts
Your power is more than we can conceive
Yet you are here with us now
You are present in this present moment
Grant us, in your grace, a glimpse of glory

HIDDEN GOD

Lord, give me the wisdom to seek you.
Though you are always with me,
I am often far from you in my thoughts.
You have come to me but I have closed
My heart and my mind to your presence.
Lord, grant that I may know you
In all things, in all people, and in my life.

Hidden God, let me seek you in and through
    creation,
Let me meet you in my acceptance of others,
Let me find you in the depth of my being.
Let me never cease to discover you,
Here and with us now,
And so be transfigured by your love,
And behold, in the world, your glory.

CHRIST ASCENDED

Christ you descended
That we might ascend
You came down
To lift us up
You faced death
To bring us to life.

Lord, raise me up:
Out of my ignorance
To an awareness of you;
Out of my darkness
Into your light;
Out of my fears
Into your protection;
Out of my loneliness
Into the fullness of your presence.

GOD UPHOLDING ALL

YOU UPHOLD ME

Holy God, Holy and Strong One,
You are with me in the darkness,
You stand beside me in each danger,
You do not leave me to my troubles.

Holy God, Holy and Strong One,
You uphold me when I am down,
You bring strength to my weakness,
You give me hope in my illness.

Holy God, Holy and Strong One,
You are there when I am afraid,
You stand beside me at death,
You raise me up to life eternal.

Holy God, Holy and Strong One,
Open my eyes to your presence,
Touch my heart with your love,
Lighten my mind with your radiance.

YOU KEEP US FROM FALLING

Lord, beneath us, you are our support.
You hold us in your arms
And keep us from falling into nothingness.
You sustain us by your power
And raise us up when we fall.
You are there when we sink into sin,
Or slide into sorrow.
When we descend to the grave,
When we face nothingness,
You raise us to newness of life
And forgive us our sins.
Enfold us in your love, O Lord,
And bring us to light eternal
To dwell safely in your care.

LORD, YOUR HAND HOLDS ME

Lord, your hand holds me,
Your love enfolds me,
Your eye beholds me.
When I stumble you support me.
When I fall you encourage me.
When I am hard-pressed you deliver me:
    From chaos and emptiness;
    From loneliness and lifelessness;
    From darkness and dreadfulness;
    From weakness and weariness;
    From failure and fearfulness.
Lord, your hand holds me,
Your love enfolds me,
Your eye beholds me.

I COMMEND MY LIFE

Lord God, my redeemer and friend,
It is you who gives me strength and courage to live.
When I am low, you raise me up.
When I am lost, you lead me forward.
When I am weak, you comfort and encourage me.
When I am troubled, you touch me with your peace.
In your hands alone is fullness of life.
In you alone is life eternal.
Into yours hands, O God,
I commend my life.

YOU MAKE ALL THINGS NEW

God, you make all things new.

When we are worn and weary,
You uphold us in your strength.
When we are cold and insensitive,
You uphold us in your love.
When we are hard and unfeeling,
You uphold us in your mercy.

When we are sore and wounded,
You renew us by your healing.
When we are trapped and imprisoned,
You renew us in your freedom.
When we are lonely and loveless,
You renew us by your presence.

Lord, we place our lives in your hands:
Remould us in your image.
Reshape us in your love.

God, you make all things new.

WHEN LIFE FALLS APART

God, when life falls apart
You pick up the pieces
And refashion them in your love.
You breathe into me new life
And renew my hope and courage.
No matter how great the darkness,
I cannot fall out of your care:
Your nail-marked hands
Seek to raise me up,
Free me from the depths
Of despair or the darkest hell,
Lift me into the fullness of life,
Guide me into your light,
And bring me to your glory.

A JOY FOR LIFE

In your hands, Lord, is life in its fullness.
Lord, my stronghold, give me strength,
With strength, give me courage,
With courage, a questing spirit
With that spirit, a joy for life,
With that joy, a love of existence,
With that love, an awareness of you,
With that awareness, your deep peace.
In that peace, let me rest in you,
And resting in you, rejoice.

THE HANDS OF GOD

Father, in the darkest night
You hold me fast in your care
Your tender hand caresses me
Your strong hand upholds me
Your loving arms enfold me

Christ, in the greatest depths
You are there right beside me
Your nailed hands save me
Your healing hands restore me
You embrace and accept me

Spirit, in the lifeless place
Your mighty hand remakes me
Your gentle hand empowers me
Your guiding hand directs me
Your presence is all around me

Holy Three, I place my hand in yours
For you are a ready help to me
Blessed Trinity, I place my life in yours,
For you, in love, reach out to me

Glory to you,
Three in One
One in Three.

GOD WITHIN ME

GOD, IN THE DAWNING

God, in the dawning
God, in the first light
God, in the sunset
God, in the night
God, in each joy
God, in each sorrow
God, in this moment
God, in tomorrow
God, in fulfilment
God, in each need
God, in my resting
God, in each deed
God, in my life
God, in my breath
God, in great love
God, in my death
God, in my rising
God, in great power
God, ever upraising
God, my strong tower

TOTAL IMMERSION

I am baptized,
I am immersed,
In the name of God:
In the presence of the Creator,
In the peace of the Saviour,
In the power of the Spirit,
In the Three and in the One.
I dwell in God and God is in me.

I am baptized,
I am immersed,
In the name of God:
In the goodness of the Father,
In the grace of the Lord Jesus,
In the guiding of the Holy Spirit,
In the Three and in the One.
I dwell in God and God is in me.

I am baptized,
I am immersed,
In the name of God:
In the love of the Father.
In the light of Christ my Lord,
In the leading of the Holy Spirit.
In the Three and in the One.
I dwell in God and God is in me.

I am baptized,
I am immersed,
In the name of God:
In the strength of the Father,
In the salvation of Christ,

In the seeking of the Spirit,
In the Three and in the One.
I dwell in God and God is in me.

I am baptized,
I am immersed,
In the name of God:
I am in God and God is in me.
As I was yesterday,
I am today,
I will be tomorrow.
In the name of the Three,
In the Holy Trinity,
Now and in eternity,
I dwell in God and God is in me.

ABIDING IN ME

God the Creator
God of Mystery
God immortal
Abiding in me

God all-loving
God of Mystery
God all-powerful
Abiding in me

God invisible
God of Mystery
God ever present
Abiding in me

ALWAYS WITH ME

God, always with me:
In my going out,
In my coming in,
In my waking,
In my sleeping,
Always with me.

In my working,
In my resting,
In life's fullness,
In life's waning,
Always with me.

In my thinking,
In my speaking,
In my silence,
In my laughing,
Always with me.

In my crying,
In my rejoicing,
In my sorrow,
In my living,
In my dying,
Always with me.

THE THREE WITH ME

The Three who are with me
The Three who are over me
The Three who are in me

The Three who are under me
The Three who surround me
The Three who are in me

The Three who protect me
The Three who guide me
The Three who are in me

The Three who abide in me
Glory to you, Holy Three
The Three who are in me

IN ME NOW

Lord, you are.
Lord, you are here, in this very moment.
Lord, you are around me and within me.
You may be unseen, yet you are very near.
You made me, love me and are within me.
You are my light, Lord, no matter how dark the day.
You are the light, Lord, that cannot be overcome.
You are the light of my life and the light in my life.
Lord, abiding in me, you are my salvation.
With you in me and I in you
I shall not perish but have everlasting life.
Lord, you are here, in this very moment.
Lord, you are.

LORD, TEACH ME TO LOVE

Lord, teach me to love.
To love myself with the love you have for me:
To share that love with my dear ones,
To reach out in that love to others,
To radiate that love to all that I meet.
Lord, teach me to love.

Lord, you reveal your love to me.
In all things and through all things.
Lord, help me to love you
Through your creation and through others,
To love you in loving my loved ones,
To give my love to you
In my care for the poor and needy,
To reveal your love
By the way I welcome strangers,
To glory in your love
By the way I live my life.
Lord, I seek to give my love to you,
Knowing that you always love me.

INDWELLING LORD

Indwelling Lord,
Be my strength
Through each day.
Wisdom of God
Scatter the darkness
Of my ignorance.
Christ my Lord,
Rule in my heart
And in this world.
Root of Jesse's stem,
Make all us one with you
As you share our humanity.
Key of David,
Unlock me from my sin
And open for me life eternal.
Bright Morning Star,
Dispel the clouds of night
And bring me to eternal day.
King of the Gentiles,
We are one in you:
Let us live in your peace.
Emmanuel, God with us,
You are here with me now
And I rejoice in your love.

ON GIVING A CANDLE

Look to God and be radiant,
Let your life be illuminated by him.
Let your mind be enlightened,
Your night become clear as the day,
And your way be guided by him.
Let God's light dawn in your heart:
Become part of that light
And radiate it to your loved ones.
Bring his light to your neighbours
And disperse the darkness around them.
Let God's light shine in your heart,
In your eyes, in your face and in your deeds.
Let it shine in the evening of your life
That it may be as bright as the noonday.
The Lord be your everlasting light.

GOD WITHIN OTHERS

GOD OF SURPRISES

God of surprises and disguises,
You wait for us to seek you,
To find you in the midst of life.
We may meet you in the crying of a child,
In an old woman needing help;
Or when held in the arms of a loved one,
Who is kissing us with their lips.
You are found in tears and laughter,
In our reaching to the stars,
Or bending to gaze at a snowdrop.
God of surprises, you wait
For us to discover you, incarnate,
In our daily acts and our daily lives.

ONE IN HIM

God, in being one with you
We are one with each other.
You are in the other person
And through them speak to me.
By attending to the other,
Help me to grow in your love.
God, it is in you alone
That can we reflect the unity
That belongs to all creation.
We are one in you
And you, Holy One, are in us.

FOUND AMONG US

Lord, help us to live in harmony:
Trusting each other and not mistrusting,
Loving one another and not hating,
Accepting one another and not rejecting,
Respecting one another and not misusing,
Attentive to one another and not ignoring,
Ready to serve one another and not domineering:
That we may see you in those we meet,
That we may meet you in our encounters with
    others,
And rejoice that you are found among us.

LORD, MAKE ME ATTENTIVE

Lord, teach me to listen,
To attend to whoever speaks.
For in the voices of friends and strangers,
In the voices of the daily news,
You speak to me.
Make me attentive to each word
That I may be open to your Word.
Teach me that in focusing on another
You give me the opportunity of meeting
You, the great Other, dwelling within.
Lord, grant me an awareness of you in others,
And may others see you in me.
And when words fail and communication breaks
    down,
May I know that you are still with every one of us
Holding us together in your heart.
Assure me that we are one in you, Lord,
And that we dwell in your never-failing love.

SEVEN DIRECTIONS, FOR INTERCESSIONS

Facing the east, the place of the dawn

Praise to you, O God, for the gift of this new morning.
Bless all who are rejoicing in newness of life today:
All who are meeting new people and facing new
   opportunities:
Families where there is a new birth,
Couples celebrating new relationships,
Children going to new schools or classes,
People making new friends,
All in new employment.

Bless all who are creating new things:
All artists, poets, writers and musicians,
All research workers and scientists,
All those planting new crops and reaping new harvests,
All cooks and bakers and those who provide us
   with food.

Bless all who are moving to new homes or jobs,
All entering into new ventures or adventures.
Blessed are you, Father, Son and Holy Spirit,
May we know that you are with each of us
In all our new beginnings, today and always.

*Facing the south, the direction of noon and the
   fullness of the day*

Blessed are you, Lord God,
Creator, who provides us with all there is.
Bless all who are making the most of their hands
   and minds,

God within others

All who are delighting in their talents,
And all who are seeing their skills develop.
Bless all who teach and educate others,
All who train people to discover their potential.

Guide with your wisdom
All who work in our cities,
All involved in government and commerce,
All who seek peace and labour for it,
All who maintain the fabric of our world.

Bless all who are in the fullness of life,
All who are employed and those they work for,
All who seek for fair trade and justice,
All who work to safeguard and restore our
    resources,
All who work in the leisure industry.
Blessed are you, Father, Son and Holy Spirit,
As the giver of all our gifts and abilities
You are always with us in the midst of life.

Facing the west and the oncoming darkness

Blessed are you, Lord our God,
You are with us in difficulty and tragedy.
Bless all who are finding life disturbing:
All whose lives are threatened by poverty or famine,
All who are deeply in debt,
All who are being made redundant,
All who are facing unemployment.

God, you surround with your love
All who suffer from criminal acts,
All facing tyranny or violence,
All who have been betrayed,

All who have been deserted,
All who are broken or broken-hearted,
All who can no longer trust others,
All who feel unable to trust in you.
Blessed are you, Father, Son and Holy Spirit,
For you are our strength and salvation
And a very present help in our troubles.
Blessed be God for ever.

Facing the north where the light disappears

Blessed are you, Lord God, creator of day and night
The darkness is no darkness with you.
Bless, O God, all entering a time when light seems
absent,
All who are terminally ill and their anxious loved
ones,
All experiencing the waning of powers,
Those losing mobility or agility,
Those whose minds can no longer cope.

Strengthen, O God of love and peace,
Those whose lives are diminished by tyranny
Those who are belittled by oppression,
Those restricted by injustice, and all who are in
captivity.

Look in mercy, O God, on
The poor of our world,
The starving and the impoverished,
The refugees and the homeless,
All who are orphaned and widowed.

Lord of life and light, you surround
All entering into the shadow of death

And all who will die this day:
May they know your love and trust in you.
Blessed are you, Lord our God,
Giver of life and light eternal

Bowing down and touching the earth

Blessed are you, Lord our God, creator of this earth.
Underneath us are your everlasting arms;
You enfold the world in your love.

Bless all who stumble and fall today:
All who tumble into sin,
All who choose the wrong path,
All who ignore advice or are misguided,
All who get into trouble in any way.

God, guide and uplift
All injured through a fall,
All whose pride feels hurt,
All who have no helpers
All who have been brought down.
God, give your strength and light to
All who despair or are depressed or suicidal,
All who feel misunderstood,
All who feel utterly alone.
Blessed are you, Lord our God,
For in Christ you came down that we might arise
    with you.
Blessed are you, Father, Son and Holy Spirit.

Raising your arms and eyes upwards

Blessed are you, eternal God.
We lift up our hearts to you,
God above us, but not beyond us.

In the chances and changes of life,
You abide with us in love and light.

Lord, you never leave us or forsake us,
Raise our sights and renew our vision
In the midst of this troubled life
Teach us to rest in your eternal changelessness.
Help us to see, as we have come from you,
We will return to you and to your love.
Let your gift of eternal life give meaning to our days;
In you we shall find lasting peace and hope.

Bless all who have departed this life,
All who are now in the fullness of your kingdom.
Bless all your saints in glory.
Give strength to all who seek to arise today,
So they can take on new challenges, overcome
    difficulties,
And rise above all that would bring them down.
Blessed be God, giver of life eternal.
Blessed be God for ever.

Placing your hand over your heart

Blessed are you, God of love,
You are in each and every one of us.
Bless those whom we shall meet today:
Our families and our friends,
Our workmates and fellow travellers.
Lord, may we see you and serve you
Through people in shops and on the streets;
Through all whom we shall influence
And all who will influence us;
Through those who need our help
And those who need our love;

Through those who will be a strength to us
And those who enfold us in their love.
God be known in the heart of all whom we meet.

Blessed are you, Lord our God,
Within us and about us.
May we be aware of you in our lives
And respond to your love for us.
Blessed are you, Father, Son and Holy Spirit.
Blessed be God for ever.

GOD WITHIN ALL CREATION

HE FILLS ALL

God, who created me,
Calls me to awaken
To his presence
Around me and within me.
His abiding presence
Is within all of creation:
In every blade of grass,
In the sun that shines,
In the winds that blow,
In the dust of the earth,
In the shimmering of the sea,
In the whiteness of the snow,
In the glory of the harvest,
In all forms of life,
In every single human being.
He is in all.
He fills all.

THE GIFT OF WONDER

Lord, give me the gift of wonder,
That rather than seek for more wonders,
I see the extraordinary
In that which is called the ordinary.
May I be aware of you indwelling in all things
And your presence in everyone I meet.
Lord, be a light to my eyes, my mind, my heart,
That I may live in a wonder-full world,
And see and radiate your glory.

GOD, TEACH ME TO LOVE

God, teach me to love the world
with the love you have for it.
Not to detach myself from others
But to encourage those around me.
Not to turn my back on this life
But to enter more deeply into it
For you are to be found
Within the world and around it:
You are present in the present.
Help me never to reject those I meet
But to accept them as you do.
For if I do not give myself to another,
I fail to give myself to you.
God, teach me to love.

HIDDEN GOD

Within each piece of creation,
within each person,
hidden God you wait
to surprise us with your glory.

Within each moment of time,
within each day and hour,
hidden God you approach us,
calling our name to make us your own.

Within each human heart,
within our innermost being,
hidden God you touch us,
awaken us and reveal your love.

Everything, everyone is within you,
all space, all time and every person:
hidden God help us to open
our eyes and our hearts to your presence.

LORD, MAKE ME AWARE

Lord, I seek to be aware of you
Wherever life takes me:
Grant me a consciousness of your presence.
In whatever I am doing, in all that I see,
Give me a glimpse of your glory.
Grant me a feeling of reverence
Towards whoever I meet;
Give me a sense of awe
In all that life reveals to me;
That I may rejoice in you
And my life show forth your praise.

THE POWER OF THE PRESENCE

Encompassing God, you are
Rest for the weary,
Strength for the weak,
Peace for the troubled,
Calm for the anxious,
Hope for the wanderer,
Love for the lonely,
Help for the sick,
Healing for the wounded,
Courage for the fearful.
Encompassing God, you are
With each of us now.
We ask you to bless ....
And enfold us in your love.

UNAWARE

Lord, I have been looking for you,
Not realizing that you are already with me.
I sought you in books and lectures.
I sought you in churches,
Unaware that you were in all things.

When you tried to talk to me,
I spoke too much in my prayers:
When you asked me to be still,
I ran around, still searching for you.

I sought your dwelling place,
Not knowing that I dwell in you
And that you abide in me.

You enfold me in your love
And encompass my days.
All there is dwells in your presence:
You are found in all things.

Lord, teach me to be still,
To rest and rejoice in you.

LORD, LET ME DISCOVER YOU

Lord, let me discover you today
In the wonders of your creation
In the animate and the inanimate
In the weak and the strong
In the young and the old
In the joyful and the sorrowing
In the saint and the sinner
In the living and the departed

Your presence is to be found in all
Though nothing can fully contain you

Lord, open the eyes of my heart
That I may see the world vibrant
With your presence and glory

BEYOND IN OUR MIDST

Creating God, I adore you.
You are found in all your creation,
In each star, each leaf, each snowflake,
In each animal and in each human being.
You fill all yet nothing can fully contain you.
You have made us and are one with us,
Yet no one can fully comprehend you.
You abide with us, you guide us,
You enfold us and dwell with us,
Yet no one can fully apprehend you.

You are known and held by our love.
Lord, may we seek to love you as you love us.
Creating God, I adore you.

THE LOVE OF GOD ENFOLDING

The love of God enfolding me
The love of God rolling free
The love of God flow out through me

Love for creation and for each creature
Love for the earth and for each feature
The love of God flow out through me

Love for my family and for my friends
Love for each one, whatever life sends
The love of God flow out through me

Love for the poor and for the stranger
Love reaching out in times of danger
The love of God flow out through me

Love for myself, created by thee
Love that redeems and is setting me free
The love of God flow out through me

TO LOVE YOUR WORLD

God you created us
To enjoy the earth,
To love your world.
Our salvation is bound up
With all of creation
And we cannot be saved alone.
We belong to the elements
From which you created us;
To destroy the earth
Is to destroy ourselves.
We need to love the world
With the love that you have
For each piece of creation.
You ask us to garden
What is already here,
Not to seek elsewhere
For another world or life.
You ask us to see the world
Radiant with your presence:
A world transfigured,
A world full of your glory,
That your kingdom come
On earth as it is in heaven.

GOD ENCOMPASSING ALL

GOD AROUND ME

God around me
God before me
God behind me
God on my right
God on my left

God above me
God under me
God within me
God on my right
God on my left

God in all I meet
God in all people
God all about us
God on my right
God on my left

AN EXERCISE IN AWARENESS

God, creator of all that there is,
who is, who was, and will always be;
God beyond all yet within all,
here with me now.

Face the east; raise your hands in praise
For rising to a new day
For rising to newness of life

God, in the beginning of all creation.
God, in the beginning of life.
God, in the beginning of the day.
God, in the beginning of each act.
God, in the beginning of each thought.
God, in each birth and rebirth.
God, in the renewal of life.

Turn to the south and rejoice in the fullness of life

God, in the high noon.
God, in the fullness of life.
God, in the flowering of my being.
God, in all that is dexterous.
God, in all my work.
God, in all achievement.
God, in the labourer and the craftsperson.

Turn to the west, offering your life to God

God, at all endings.
God, at the eve of the day.
God, at the close of life.
God, at my back to protect me.

God, forgiving my sins.
God, saving me from all evil.
God, keeping me in your power.

*Turn to the north and dedicate all troubles and
   darkness to God*

God, in the darkness.
God, in the depths of life.
God, even when I cannot see you.
God, in deep places of my being.
God, in the sinister.
God, triumphing over evil.
God, always there.
God, unseen yet ever near.

Touch the earth or be aware of it beneath you

God, beneath me.
God, your hand to hold me.
God, to uphold me.
God, to support me.
God, to sustain me.
God, to save me.
Help me to remember you made the earth
That I am part of its creation and well-being.

Look up to the heights and lift up your heart

God, above me.
God, to uplift me.
God, to raise my sights.
God, in my hopes and my ideals.
God, you are the beyond in our midst.
God, to you be the glory.

Place your hands over your heart or chest

God, you are within me.
God, to be discovered in my life.
God, to be found within all things.
God, within this day.
God, within each part of creation.
God, within and about me.
God, in my heart.
God, in meeting with friend or stranger.

ENFOLDED IN LOVE

God, you encompass us
With the radiance of your presence:
You enfold us in your love.
Lord, set our lives aflame with your glory
That we may shine with your goodness
And love you with all our heart, all our mind
All our soul and all our strength.
And love our neighbours
As you love us.

GOD YOU ARE

God, you are
God, you are here
God, you are with me now

You encompass me
You abide with me
In your presence is peace
In your presence is love
In your presence is joy
In your presence is life eternal

God, you are with me now
God, you are here
God, you are

ALWAYS THERE

In times of darkness
In times of stress
Lord, you are there
Always there

In times of tempest
In times of shock
Lord, you are there
Always there

In times of anxiety
In times of doubt
Lord, you are there
Always there

In times of loneliness
In times of despair
Lord, you are there
Always there

In times of celebration
In times of joy
Lord, you are there
Always there

In times of emptiness
In times of plenty
Lord, you are there
Always there

MY GOD ENCIRCLING ME

My God, my light, my love, encompassing me.
My strength, my shield, my support, enfolding me.
Each day and night, each dark, each light,
My God, my light, my love, encompassing me.

My God, my grace, my guide, encircling me.
My helper, my upholder, my joy, surrounding me.
Each day, each night, each dark, each light,
My God, my grace, my guide, encircling me.

My God, abiding within me and about me:
In my waking, in my working and in my sleeping
In my activity, in my thinking and in my resting
My God, abiding within me and about me.

GOD WITH US

God, you are with us
God, you encompass us
God, you are all around us
God, you never leave us
God, you go with us
God, you guide us
God, you strengthen us
God, you are about us
God, you abide within us
Alleluia!

THE HOLY THREE

Encircled by the Holy Three,
Enclosed within the Trinity.
All around me at this hour
Is the Lord's almighty power.
The Father's strength with grace upholds.
The Son's deep love with warmth enfolds.
The Spirit's light shines clear to guide.
Encircled by the Holy Three,
Enclosed within the Trinity

Day and night I know I'll be
Surrounded by the Trinity.
The Father ever loving me.
The Son ever saving me.
The Spirit ever leading me.
Encircled by the Holy Three,
Enclosed within the Trinity

I rejoice now in the Holy Three,
Their presence all about me:
God's eye to watch, his hand to hold
His ear to hear, his heart to love.
Encircled by the Holy Three
Enclosed within the Trinity

DEEP MYSTERY

Holy Three
Deep mystery
Surrounding me
One in Three
Protecting me
The Father be
Upholding me
The Saviour be
Forgiving me
The Spirit be
Strength to me
The Holy Three
Defending me
As night does fall
Bless one and all
As the shadows fall
God hear my call
The Sacred Three
Encircling me
So let it be
Amen to thee
Holy Three
About me